The Oxford India Paper Dickens, Copyright Edition
With Illustrations by Cruikshank, 'Phiz,' &c.
In Seventeen Volumes

Christmas Stories

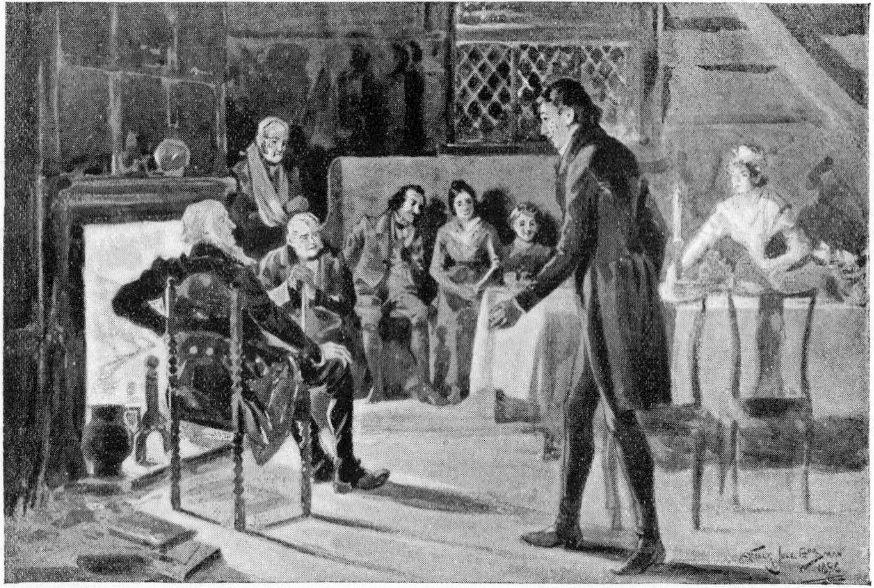

THE SEVEN POOR TRAVELLERS

Christmas Stories

from

"Household Words"

&

"All the Year Round"

By

Charles Dickens

With Eight Illustrations
By A. Jules Goodman

London
Chapman & Hall, Limited; and
Henry Frowde
New York: Oxford University Press American Branch
91 & 93 Fifth Avenue

Printed by HORACE HART
University Press, Oxford

CONTENTS

LIST OF ILLUSTRATIONS

A CHRISTMAS TREE

[1850]

A CHRISTMAS TREE

I HAVE been looking on, this evening, at a merry company of children assembled round that pretty German toy, a Christmas Tree. The tree was planted in the middle of a great round table, and towered high above their heads. It was brilliantly lighted by a multitude of little tapers; and everywhere sparkled and glittered with bright objects. There were rosy-cheeked dolls, hiding behind the green leaves; and there were real watches (with movable hands, at least, and an endless capacity of being wound up) dangling from innumerable twigs; there were French-polished tables, chairs, bedsteads, wardrobes, eight-day clocks, and various other articles of domestic furniture (wonderfully made, in tin, at Wolverhampton), perched among the boughs, as if in preparation for some fairy housekeeping; there were jolly, broad-faced little men, much more agreeable in appearance than many real men—and no wonder, for their heads took off, and showed them to be full of sugar-plums; there were fiddles and drums; there were tambourines, books, work-boxes, paint-boxes, sweetmeat boxes, peep-show boxes, and all kinds of boxes; there were trinkets for the elder girls, far brighter than any grown-up gold and jewels; there were baskets and pincushions in all devices; there were guns, swords, and banners; there were witches standing in enchanted rings of pasteboard, to tell fortunes; there were tee-totums, humming-tops, needle-cases, pen-wipers, smelling-bottles, conversation-cards, bouquet-holders; real fruit, made artificially dazzling with gold leaf; imitation apples, pears, and walnuts, crammed with surprises; in short, as a pretty child, before me, delightedly whispered to another pretty child, her bosom friend, "There was everything, and more." This motley collection of odd objects, clustering on the tree

like magic fruit, and flashing back the bright looks directed
towards it from every side—some of the diamond-eyes ad-
miring it were hardly on a level with the table, and a few
were languishing in timid wonder on the bosoms of pretty
mothers, aunts, and nurses—made a lively realisation of the
fancies of childhood ; and set me thinking how all the trees
that grow and all the things that come into existence on the
earth, have their wild adornments at that well-remembered
time.

Being now at home again, and alone, the only person in
the house awake, my thoughts are drawn back, by a fasci-
nation which I do not care to resist, to my own childhood.
I begin to consider, what do we all remember best upon the
branches of the Christmas Tree of our own young Christmas
days, by which we climbed to real life.

Straight, in the middle of the room, cramped in the free-
dom of its growth by no encircling walls or soon-reached
ceiling, a shadowy tree arises ; and, looking up into the
dreamy brightness of its top—for I observe in this tree the
singular property that it appears to grow downward towards
the earth—I look into my youngest Christmas recollections !

All toys at first, I find. Up yonder, among the green holly
and red berries, is the Tumbler with his hands in his pockets,
who wouldn't lie down, but whenever he was put upon the
floor, persisted in rolling his fat body about, until he rolled
himself still, and brought those lobster eyes of his to bear
upon me—when I affected to laugh very much, but in my
heart of hearts was extremely doubtful of him.   Close beside
him is that infernal snuff-box, out of which there sprang a
demoniacal Counsellor in a black gown, with an obnoxious
head of hair, and a red cloth mouth, wide open, who was
not to be endured on any terms, but could not be put away
either ; for he used suddenly, in a highly magnified state, to
fly out of Mammoth Snuff-boxes in dreams, when least expected.   Nor is the frog with cobbler's wax on his tail, far
off ; for there was no knowing where he wouldn't jump ; and
when he flew over the candle, and came upon one's hand
with that spotted back—red on a green ground—he was
horrible. The cardboard lady in a blue-silk skirt, who was
stood up against the candlestick to dance, and whom I see
on the same branch, was milder, and was beautiful ; but I
can't say as much for the larger cardboard man, who used
to be hung against the wall and pulled by a string ; there

was a sinister expression in that nose of his; and when he got his legs round his neck (which he very often did), he was ghastly, and not a creature to be alone with.

When did that dreadful Mask first look at me? Who put it on, and why was I so frightened that the sight of it is an era in my life? It is not a hideous visage in itself; it is even meant to be droll; why then were its stolid features so intolerable? Surely not because it hid the wearer's face. An apron would have done as much; and though I should have preferred even the apron away, it would not have been absolutely insupportable, like the mask. Was it the immovability of the mask? The doll's face was immovable, but I was not afraid of *her*. Perhaps that fixed and set change coming over a real face, infused into my quickened heart some remote suggestion and dread of the universal change that is to come on every face, and make it still? Nothing reconciled me to it. No drummers, from whom proceeded a melancholy chirping on the turning of a handle; no regiment of soldiers, with a mute band, taken out of a box, and fitted, one by one, upon a stiff and lazy little set of lazy-tongs; no old woman, made of wires and a brown-paper composition, cutting up a pie for two small children; could give me a permanent comfort, for a long time. Nor was it any satisfaction to be shown the Mask, and see that it was made of paper, or to have it locked up and be assured that no one wore it. The mere recollection of that fixed face, the mere knowledge of its existence anywhere, was sufficient to awake me in the night all perspiration and horror, with, "O I know it's coming! O the mask!"

I never wondered what the dear old donkey with the panniers—there he is! was made of, then! His hide was real to the touch, I recollect. And the great black horse with the round red spots all over him—the horse that I could even get upon—I never wondered what had brought him to that strange condition, or thought that such a horse was not commonly seen at Newmarket. The four horses of no colour, next to him, that went into the waggon of cheeses, and could be taken out and stabled under the piano, appear to have bits of fur-tippet for their tails, and other bits for their manes, and to stand on pegs instead of legs, but it was not so when they were brought home for a Christmas present. They were all right, then; neither was their harness unceremoniously nailed into their chests, as appears to be the case now. The tinkling works of the music-cart, I *did* find out, to be made of quill toothpicks and wire; and I always thought that little tumbler in his shirt-sleeves, perpetually swarming up one side of a wooden frame, and coming down, head foremost, on the other, rather a weak-minded person—though good-natured; but the Jacob's Ladder, next him, made of little squares of red wood, that went flapping and clattering over one another, each developing a different picture, and the whole enlivened by small bells, was a mighty marvel and a great delight.

Ah! The Doll's house!—of which I was not proprietor, but where I visited. I don't admire the Houses of Parliament half so much as that stone-fronted mansion with real glass windows, and doorsteps, and a real balcony—greener than I ever see now, except at watering places; and even they afford but a poor imitation. And though it *did* open all at once, the entire house-front (which was a blow, I admit, as cancelling the fiction of a staircase), it was but to shut it up again, and I could believe. Even open, there were three distinct rooms in it: a sitting-room and bed-room, elegantly furnished, and best of all, a kitchen, with uncommonly soft fire-irons, a plentiful assortment of diminutive utensils—oh, the warming-pan!—and a tin man-cook in profile, who was always going to fry two fish. What Barmecide justice have I done to the noble feasts wherein the set of wooden platters figured, each with its own peculiar delicacy, as a ham or turkey, glued tight on to it, and garnished with something green, which I recollect as moss! Could all the Temperance Societies of these later days, united, give me such a tea-drinking as I have had through the means of yonder little set of blue crockery, which really would hold liquid (it ran out of the small wooden cask, I recollect, and tasted of matches), and which made tea, nectar. And if the two legs of the ineffectual little sugar-tongs did tumble over one another, and want purpose, like Punch's hands, what does it matter? And if I did once shriek out, as a poisoned child, and strike the fashionable company with consternation, by reason of having drunk a little teaspoon, inadvertently dissolved in too hot tea, I was never the worse for it, except by a powder!

Upon the next branches of the tree, lower down, hard by the green roller and miniature gardening-tools, how thick the books begin to hang. Thin books, in themselves, at first, but

many of them, and with deliciously smooth covers of bright
red or green. What fat black letters to begin with ! "A
was an archer, and shot at a frog." Of course he was. He
was an apple-pie also, and there he is ! He was a good many
things in his time, was A, and so were most of his friends,
except X, who had so little versatility, that I never knew him
to get beyond Xerxes or Xantippe—like Y, who was always
confined to a Yacht or a Yew Tree ; and Z condemned for
ever to be a Zebra or a Zany. But, now, the very tree itself
changes, and becomes a bean-stalk—the marvellous bean-stalk
up which Jack climbed to the Giant's house ! And now, those
dreadfully interesting, double-headed giants, with their clubs
over their shoulders, begin to stride along the boughs in a
perfect throng, dragging knights and ladies home for dinner
by the hair of their heads. And Jack—how noble, with his
sword of sharpness, and his shoes of swiftness ! Again those
old meditations come upon me as I gaze up at him ; and I
debate within myself whether there was more than one Jack
(which I am loth to believe possible), or only one genuine
original admirable Jack, who achieved all the recorded
exploits.

Good for Christmas-time is the ruddy colour of the cloak,
in which—the tree making a forest of itself for her to trip
through, with her basket—Little Red Riding-Hood comes to
me one Christmas Eve to give me information of the cruelty
and treachery of that dissembling Wolf who ate her grand-
mother, without making any impression on his appetite, and
then ate her, after making that ferocious joke about his teeth.
She was my first love. I felt that if I could have married
Little Red Riding-Hood, I should have known perfect bliss.
But, it was not to be ; and there was nothing for it but to look
out the Wolf in the Noah's Ark there, and put him late in the
procession on the table, as a monster who was to be degraded.
O the wonderful Noah's Ark ! It was not found seaworthy
when put in a washing-tub, and the animals were crammed in
at the roof, and needed to have their legs well shaken down
before they could be got in, even there—and then, ten to one
but they began to tumble out at the door, which was but
imperfectly fastened with a wire latch—but what was *that*
against it ! Consider the noble fly, a size or two smaller than
the elephant : the lady-bird, the butterfly—all triumphs of
art ! Consider the goose, whose feet were so small, and whose
balance was so indifferent, that he usually tumbled forward,

and knocked down all the animal creation. Consider Noah
and his family, like idiotic tobacco-stoppers; and how the
leopard stuck to warm little fingers; and how the tails of
the larger animals used gradually to resolve themselves into
frayed bits of string!

Hush! Again a forest, and somebody up in a tree—not
Robin Hood, not Valentine, not the Yellow Dwarf (I have
passed him and all Mother Bunch's wonders, without men-
tion), but an Eastern King with a glittering scimitar and
turban. By Allah! two Eastern Kings, for I see another,
looking over his shoulder! Down upon the grass, at the tree's
foot, lies the full length of a coal-black Giant, stretched
asleep, with his head in a lady's lap; and near them is
a glass box, fastened with four locks of shining steel, in which
he keeps the lady prisoner when he is awake. I see the four
keys at his girdle now. The lady makes signs to the two
kings in the tree, who softly descend. It is the setting-in of
the bright Arabian Nights.

Oh, now all common things become uncommon and enchanted to me. All lamps are wonderful; all rings are
talismans. Common flower-pots are full of treasure, with a
little earth scattered on the top; trees are for Ali Baba to
hide in; beefsteaks are to throw down into the Valley of
Diamonds, that the precious stones may stick to them, and be
carried by the eagles to their nests, whence the traders, with
loud cries, will scare them. Tarts are made, according to the
recipe of the Vizier's son of Bussorah, who turned pastrycook
after he was set down in his drawers at the gate of Damascus;
cobblers are all Mustaphas, and in the habit of sewing up
people cut into four pieces, to whom they are taken blind-
fold.

Any iron ring let into stone is the entrance to a cave which
only waits for the magician, and the little fire, and the
necromancy, that will make the earth shake. All the dates
imported come from the same tree as that unlucky date, with
whose shell the merchant knocked out the eye of the genie's
invisible son. All olives are of the stock of that fresh fruit,
concerning which the Commander of the Faithful overheard
the boy conduct the fictitious trial of the fraudulent olive
merchant; all apples are akin to the apple purchased (with
two others) from the Sultan's gardener for three sequins, and
which the tall black slave stole from the child. All dogs are
associated with the dog, really a transformed man, who

jumped upon the baker's counter, and put his paw on the piece of bad money. All rice recalls the rice which the awful lady, who was a ghoule, could only peck by grains, because of her nightly feasts in the burial-place. My very rocking-horse,—there he is, with his nostrils turned completely inside-out, indicative of Blood!—should have a peg in his neck, by virtue thereof to fly away with me, as the wooden horse did with the Prince of Persia, in the sight of all his father's Court.

Yes, on every object that I recognise among those upper branches of my Christmas Tree, I see this fairy light! When I wake in bed, at daybreak, on the cold dark winter mornings, the white snow dimly beheld, outside, through the frost on the window-pane, I hear Dinarzade. "Sister, sister, if you are yet awake, I pray you finish the history of the Young King of the Black Islands." Scheherazade replies, "If my lord the Sultan will suffer me to live another day, sister, I will not only finish that, but tell you a more wonderful story yet." Then, the gracious Sultan goes out, giving no orders for the execution, and we all three breathe again.

At this height of my tree I begin to see, cowering among the leaves—it may be born of turkey, or of pudding, or mince pie, or of these many fancies, jumbled with Robinson Crusoe on his desert island, Philip Quarll among the monkeys, Sandford and Merton with Mr. Barlow, Mother Bunch, and the Mask—or it may be the result of indigestion, assisted by imagination and over-doctoring—a prodigious nightmare. It is so exceedingly indistinct, that I don't know why it's frightful—but I know it is. I can only make out that it is an immense array of shapeless things, which appear to be planted on a vast exaggeration of the lazy-tongs that used to bear the toy soldiers, and to be slowly coming close to my eyes, and receding to an immeasurable distance. When it comes closest, it is worse. In connexion with it I descry remembrances of winter nights incredibly long; of being sent early to bed, as a punishment for some small offence, and waking in two hours, with a sensation of having been asleep two nights; of the laden hopelessness of morning ever dawning; and the oppression of a weight of remorse.

And now, I see a wonderful row of little lights rise smoothly out of the ground, before a vast green curtain. Now, a bell rings—a magic bell, which still sounds in my ears unlike all other bells—and music plays, amidst a buzz of voices, and a fragrant smell of orange-peel and oil. Anon, the magic bell commands the music to cease, and the great green curtain rolls itself up majestically, and The Play begins! The devoted dog of Montargis avenges the death of his master, foully murdered in the Forest of Bondy; and a humorous Peasant with a red nose and a very little hat, whom I take from this hour forth to my bosom as a friend (I think he was a Waiter or an Hostler at a village Inn, but many years have passed since he and I have met), remarks that the sassigassity of that dog is indeed surprising; and evermore this jocular conceit will live in my remembrance fresh and unfading, overtopping all possible jokes, unto the end of time. Or now, I learn with bitter tears how poor Jane Shore, dressed all in white, and with her brown hair hanging down, went starving through the streets; or how George Barnwell killed the worthiest uncle that ever man had, and was afterwards so sorry for it that he ought to have been let off. Comes swift to comfort me, the Pantomime—stupendous Phenomenon!—when clowns are shot from loaded mortars into the great chandelier, bright constellation that it is; when Harlequins, covered all over with scales of pure gold, twist and sparkle, like amazing fish; when Pantaloon (whom I deem it no irreverence to compare in my own mind to my grandfather) puts red-hot pokers in his pocket, and cries "Here's somebody coming!" or taxes the Clown with petty larceny, by saying, "Now, I sawed you do it!" when Everything is capable, with the greatest ease, of being changed into Anything; and "Nothing is, but thinking makes it so." Now, too, I perceive my first experience of the dreary sensation— often to return in after-life—of being unable, next day, to get back to the dull, settled world; of wanting to live for ever in the bright atmosphere I have quitted; of doting on the little Fairy, with the wand like a celestial Barber's Pole, and pining for a Fairy immortality along with her. Ah, she comes back, in many shapes, as my eye wanders down the branches of my Christmas Tree, and goes as often, and has never yet stayed by me!

Out of this delight springs the toy-theatre,—there it is, with its familiar proscenium, and ladies in feathers, in the boxes!—and all its attendant occupation with paste and glue, and gum, and water colours, in the getting-up of The Miller and his Men, and Elizabeth, or the Exile of Siberia. In spite of a few besetting accidents and failures (particularly an unreasonable disposition in the respectable Kelmar, and some others, to become faint in the legs, and double up, at exciting points of the drama), a teeming world of fancies so suggestive and all-embracing, that, far below it on my Christmas Tree, I see dark, dirty, real Theatres in the day-time, adorned with these associations as with the freshest garlands of the rarest flowers, and charming me yet.

But hark! The Waits are playing, and they break my childish sleep! What images do I associate with the Christmas music as I see them set forth on the Christmas Tree? Known before all the others, keeping far apart from all the others, they gather round my little bed. An angel, speaking to a group of shepherds in a field; some travellers, with eyes uplifted, following a star; a baby in a manger; a child in a spacious temple, talking with grave men; a solemn figure, with a mild and beautiful face, raising a dead girl by the hand; again, near a city gate, calling back the son of a widow, on his bier, to life; a crowd of people looking through the opened roof of a chamber where he sits, and letting down a sick person on a bed, with ropes; the same, in a tempest, walking on the water to a ship; again, on a sea-shore, teaching a great multitude; again, with a child upon his knee, and other children round; again, restoring sight to the blind, speech to the dumb, hearing to the deaf, health to the sick, strength to the lame, knowledge to the ignorant; again, dying upon a Cross, watched by armed soldiers, a thick darkness coming on, the earth beginning to shake, and only one voice heard, "Forgive them, for they know not what they do."

Still, on the lower and maturer branches of the Tree, Christmas associations cluster thick. School-books shut up; Ovid and Virgil silenced; the Rule of Three, with its cool impertinent inquiries, long disposed of; Terence and Plautus acted no more, in an arena of huddled desks and forms, all chipped, and notched, and inked; cricket-bats, stumps, and balls, left higher up, with the smell of trodden grass and the softened noise of shouts in the evening air; the tree is still fresh, still gay. If I no more come home at Christmas-time, there will be boys and girls (thank Heaven!) while the World lasts; and they do! Yonder they dance and play upon the branches of my Tree, God bless them, merrily, and my heart dances and plays too!

And I *do* come home at Christmas. We all do, or we all should. We all come home, or ought to come home, for a short holiday—the longer, the better—from the great boarding-school, where we are for ever working at our arithmetical slates, to take, and give a rest. As to going a visiting, where can we not go, if we will; where have we not been, when we would; starting our fancy from our Christmas Tree!

Away into the winter prospect. There are many such upon the tree! On, by low-lying, misty grounds, through fens and fogs, up long hills, winding dark as caverns between thick plantations, almost shutting out the sparkling stars; so, out on broad heights, until we stop at last, with sudden silence, at an avenue. The gate-bell has a deep, half-awful sound in the frosty air; the gate swings open on its hinges; and, as we drive up to a great house, the glancing lights grow larger in the windows, and the opposing rows of trees seem to fall solemnly back on either side, to give us place. At intervals, all day, a frightened hare has shot across this whitened turf; or the distant clatter of a herd of deer trampling the hard frost, has, for the minute, crushed the silence too. Their watchful eyes beneath the fern may be shining now, if we could see them, like the icy dewdrops on the leaves; but they are still, and all is still. And so, the lights growing larger, and the trees falling back before us, and closing up again behind us, as if to forbid retreat, we come to the house.

There is probably a smell of roasted chestnuts and other good comfortable things all the time, for we are telling Winter Stories—Ghost Stories, or more shame for us—round the Christmas fire; and we have never stirred, except to draw a little nearer to it. But, no matter for that. We came to the house, and it is an old house, full of great chimneys where wood is burnt on ancient dogs upon the hearth, and grim portraits (some of them with grim legends, too) lower distrustfully from the oaken panels of the walls. We are a middle-aged nobleman, and we make a generous supper with our host and hostess and their guests—it being Christmas-time, and the old house full of company—and then we go to bed. Our room is a very old room. It is hung with tapestry. We don't like the portrait of a cavalier in green, over the fireplace. There are great black beams in the ceiling, and there is a great black bedstead, supported at the foot by two great black figures, who seem to have come off a couple of tombs in the old baronial church in the park, for our particular accommodation. But, we are not a super-

stitious nobleman, and we don't mind. Well! we dismiss
our servant, lock the door, and sit before the fire in our
dressing-gown, musing about a great many things. At length
we go to bed. Well! we can't sleep. We toss and tumble,
and can't sleep. The embers on the hearth burn fitfully and
make the room look ghostly. We can't help peeping out over
the counterpane, at the two black figures and the cavalier—
that wicked-looking cavalier—in green. In the flickering
light they seem to advance and retire: which, though we are
not by any means a superstitious nobleman, is not agreeable.
Well! we get nervous—more and more nervous. We say
"This is very foolish, but we can't stand this; we'll pre-
tend to be ill, and knock up somebody." Well! we are just
going to do it, when the locked door opens, and there comes
in a young woman, deadly pale, and with long fair hair, who
glides to the fire, and sits down in the chair we have left
there, wringing her hands. Then, we notice that her clothes
are wet. Our tongue cleaves to the roof of our mouth, and
we can't speak; but, we observe her accurately. Her clothes
are wet; her long hair is dabbled with moist mud; she is
dressed in the fashion of two hundred years ago; and she
has at her girdle a bunch of rusty keys. Well! there she
sits, and we can't even faint, we are in such a state about it.
Presently she gets up, and tries all the locks in the room
with the rusty keys, which won't fit one of them; then, she
fixes her eyes on the portrait of the cavalier in green, and
says, in a low, terrible voice, "The stags know it!" After
that, she wrings her hands again, passes the bedside, and
goes out at the door. We hurry on our dressing-gown, seize
our pistols (we always travel with pistols), and are following,
when we find the door locked. We turn the key, look out
into the dark gallery; no one there. We wander away,
and try to find our servant. Can't be done. We pace the
gallery till daybreak; then return to our deserted room, fall
asleep, and are awakened by our servant (nothing ever haunts
him) and the shining sun. Well! we make a wretched breakfast, and all the company say we look queer. After breakfast,
we go over the house with our host, and then we take him to
the portrait of the cavalier in green, and then it all comes
out. He was false to a young housekeeper once attached to
that family, and famous for her beauty, who drowned herself
in a pond, and whose body was discovered, after a long time,
because the stags refused to drink of the water. Since which,

Or, the uncle of my brother's wife was riding home on horseback, one mellow evening at sunset, when, in a green lane close to his own house, he saw a man standing before him, in the very centre of a narrow way. "Why does that man in the cloak stand there?" he thought. "Does he want me to ride over him?" But the figure never moved. He felt a strange sensation at seeing it so still, but slackened his trot and rode forward. When he was so close to it, as almost to touch it with his stirrup, his horse shied, and the figure glided up the bank, in a curious, unearthly manner—backward, and without seeming to use its feet—and was gone. The uncle of my brother's wife, exclaiming, "Good Heaven! It's my cousin Harry, from Bombay!" put spurs to his horse, which was suddenly in a profuse sweat, and, wondering at such strange behaviour, dashed round to the front of his house. There, he saw the same figure, just passing in at the long French window of the drawing-room, opening on the ground. He threw his bridle to a servant, and hastened in after it. His sister was sitting there, alone. "Alice, where's my cousin Harry?" "Your cousin Harry, John?" "Yes. From Bombay. I met him in the lane just now, and saw him enter here, this instant." Not a creature had been seen by any one; and in that hour and minute, as it afterwards appeared, this cousin died in India.

Or, it was a certain sensible old maiden lady, who died at ninety-nine, and retained her faculties to the last, who really did see the Orphan Boy; a story which has often been incorrectly told, but, of which the real truth is this—because it is, in fact, a story belonging to our family—and she was a connexion of our family. When she was about forty years of age, and still an uncommonly fine woman (her lover died young, which was the reason why she never married, though she had many offers), she went to stay at a place in Kent, which her brother, an Indian-Merchant, had newly bought. There was a story that this place had once been held in trust, by the guardian of a young boy; who was himself the next heir, and who killed the young boy by harsh and cruel treatment. She knew nothing of that. It has been said that there was a Cage in her bedroom in which the guardian used to put the boy. There was no such thing. There was only a closet. She went to bed, made no alarm whatever in the night, and in the morning said composedly to her maid when she came in, "Who is the pretty forlorn-looking child

who has been peeping out of that closet all night?" The
maid replied by giving a loud scream, and instantly decamp-
ing. She was surprised; but she was a woman of remarkable
strength of mind, and she dressed herself and went down-
stairs, and closeted herself with her brother. "Now, Walter,"
she said, "I have been disturbed all night by a pretty,
forlorn-looking boy, who has been constantly peeping out of
that closet in my room, which I can't open. This is some
trick." "I am afraid not, Charlotte," said he, "for it is the
legend of the house. It is the Orphan Boy. What did he
do?" "He opened the door softly," said she, "and peeped
out. Sometimes, he came a step or two into the room. Then,
I called to him, to encourage him, and he shrunk, and
shuddered, and crept in again, and shut the door." "The
closet has no communication, Charlotte," said her brother,
"with any other part of the house, and it's nailed up."
This was undeniably true, and it took two carpenters a whole
forenoon to get it open, for examination. Then, she was
satisfied that she had seen the Orphan Boy. But, the wild
and terrible part of the story is, that he was also seen by
three of her brother's sons, in succession, who all died young.
On the occasion of each child being taken ill, he came home
in a heat, twelve hours before, and said, Oh, mama, he
had been playing under a particular oak-tree, in a certain
meadow, with a strange boy—a pretty, forlorn-looking boy,
who was very timid, and made signs! From fatal experience,
the parents came to know that this was the Orphan Boy,
and that the course of that child whom he chose for his
little playmate was surely run.

Legion is the name of the German castles, where we sit
up alone to wait for the Spectre—where we are shown into
a room, made comparatively cheerful for our reception—
where we glance round at the shadows, thrown on the blank
walls by the crackling fire—where we feel very lonely when
the village innkeeper and his pretty daughter have retired,
after laying down a fresh store of wood upon the hearth, and
setting forth on the small table such supper-cheer as a cold
roast capon, bread, grapes, and a flask of old Rhine wine—
where the reverberating doors close on their retreat, one after
another, like so many peals of sullen thunder—and where,
about the small hours of the night, we come into the knowledge of divers supernatural mysteries. Legion is the name
of the haunted German students, in whose society we draw

WHAT CHRISTMAS IS AS WE GROW OLDER

[1851]

WHAT CHRISTMAS IS AS WE GROW OLDER

*

TIME was, with most of us, when Christmas Day encircling all our limited world like a magic ring, left nothing out for us to miss or seek ; bound together all our home enjoyments, affections, and hopes ; grouped everything and every one around the Christmas fire ; and made the little picture shining in our bright young eyes, complete.

Time came, perhaps, all too soon, when our thoughts over-leaped that narrow boundary ; when there was some one (very dear, we thought then, very beautiful, and absolutely perfect) wanting to the fulness of our happiness ; when we were wanting too (or we thought so, which did just as well) at the Christmas hearth by which that some one sat ; and when we intertwined with every wreath and garland of our life that some one's name.

That was the time for the bright visionary Christmases which have long arisen from us to show faintly, after summer rain, in the palest edges of the rainbow ! That was the time for the beatified enjoyment of the things that were to be, and never were, and yet the things that were so real in our resolute hope that it would be hard to say, now, what realities achieved since, have been stronger !

What ! Did that Christmas never really come when we and the priceless pearl who was our young choice were received, after the happiest of totally impossible marriages, by the two united families previously at daggers-drawn on our account ? When brothers and sisters in law who had always been rather cool to us before our relationship was effected, perfectly doted on us, and when fathers and mothers overwhelmed us with unlimited incomes ? Was that Christmas dinner never really eaten, after which we arose, and generously and eloquently rendered honour to our late rival, present in the company, then and there exchanging friendship and forgiveness, and founding an attachment, not to be surpassed in Greek or Roman story, which subsisted until death? Has that same rival long ceased to care for that same priceless pearl, and married for money, and become usurious? Above all, do we really know, now, that we should probably have been miserable if we had won and worn the pearl, and that we are better without her?

That Christmas when we had recently achieved so much fame; when we had been carried in triumph somewhere, for doing something great and good; when we had won an honoured and ennobled name, and arrived and were received at home in a shower of tears of joy; is it possible that *that* Christmas has not come yet?

And is our life here, at the best, so constituted that, pausing as we advance at such a noticeable milestone in the track as this great birthday, we look back on the things that never were, as naturally and full as gravely as on the things that have been and are gone, or have been and still are? If it be so, and so it seems to be, must we come to the conclusion that life is little better than a dream, and little worth the loves and strivings that we crowd into it?

No! Far be such miscalled philosophy from us, dear Reader, on Christmas Day! Nearer and closer to our hearts be the Christmas spirit, which is the spirit of active usefulness, perseverance, cheerful discharge of duty, kindness and forbearance! It is in the last virtues especially, that we are, or should be, strengthened by the unaccomplished visions of our youth; for, who shall say that they are not our teachers to deal gently even with the impalpable nothings of the earth!

Therefore, as we grow older, let us be more thankful that the circle of our Christmas associations and of the lessons that they bring, expands! Let us welcome every one of them, and summon them to take their places at the Christmas hearth.

Welcome, old aspirations, glittering creatures of an ardent fancy, to your shelter underneath the holly! We know you, and have not outlived you yet. Welcome, old projects and old loves, however fleeting, to your nooks among the steadier lights that burn around us. Welcome, all that was ever real to our hearts; and for the earnestness that made you

real, thanks to Heaven! Do we build no Christmas castles
in the clouds now? Let our thoughts, fluttering like butter-
flies among these flowers of children, bear witness! Before
this boy, there stretches out a Future, brighter than we ever
looked on in our old romantic time, but bright with honour
and with truth. Around this little head on which the sunny
curls lie heaped, the graces sport, as prettily, as airily, as
when there was no scythe within the reach of Time to shear
away the curls of our first-love. Upon another girl's face
near it—placider but smiling bright—a quiet and contented
little face, we see Home fairly written. Shining from the
word, as rays shine from a star, we see how, when our graves
are old, other hopes than ours are young, other hearts than
ours are moved; how other ways are smoothed; how other
happiness blooms, ripens, and decays—no, not decays, for
other homes and other bands of children, not yet in being
nor for ages yet to be, arise, and bloom and ripen to the end
of all!

Welcome, everything! Welcome, alike what has been,
and what never was, and what we hope may be, to your
shelter underneath the holly, to your places round the Christmas fire, where what is sits open-hearted! In yonder shadow,
do we see obtruding furtively upon the blaze, an enemy's
face? By Christmas Day we do forgive him! If the injury
he has done us may admit of such companionship, let him
come here and take his place. If otherwise, unhappily, let
him go hence, assured that we will never injure nor accuse
him.

On this day we shut out Nothing!

"Pause," says a low voice. "Nothing? Think!"

"On Christmas Day, we will shut out from our fireside,
Nothing."

"Not the shadow of a vast City where the withered leaves
are lying deep?" the voice replies. "Not the shadow that
darkens the whole globe? Not the shadow of the City of
the Dead?"

Not even that. Of all days in the year, we will turn our
faces towards that City upon Christmas Day, and from its
silent hosts bring those we loved, among us. City of the
Dead, in the blessed name wherein we are gathered together
at this time, and in the Presence that is here among us according to the promise, we will receive, and not dismiss, the
people who are dear to us!

Yes. We can look upon these children angels that alight, so solemnly, so beautifully among the living children by the fire, and can bear to think how they departed from us. Entertaining angels unawares, as the Patriarchs did, the playful children are unconscious of their guests; but we can see them—can see a radiant arm around one favourite neck, as if there were a tempting of that child away. Among the celestial figures there is one, a poor mis-shapen boy on earth, of a glorious beauty now, of whom his dying mother said it grieved her much to leave him here, alone, for so many years as it was likely would elapse before he came to her—being such a little child. But he went quickly, and was laid upon her breast, and in her hand she leads him.

There was a gallant boy, who fell, far away, upon a burning sand beneath a burning sun, and said, "Tell them at home, with my last love, how much I could have wished to kiss them once, but that I died contented and had done my duty!" Or there was another, over whom they read the words, "Therefore we commit his body to the deep," and so consigned him to the lonely ocean and sailed on. Or there was another, who lay down to his rest in the dark shadow of great forests, and, on earth, awoke no more. O shall they not, from sand and sea and forest, be brought home at such a time?

There was a dear girl—almost a woman—never to be one —who made a mourning Christmas in a house of joy, and went her trackless way to the silent City. Do we recollect her, worn out, faintly whispering what could not be heard, and falling into that last sleep for weariness? O look upon her now! O look upon her beauty, her serenity, her changeless youth, her happiness! The daughter of Jairus was recalled to life, to die; but she, more blest, has heard the same voice, saying unto her, "Arise for ever!"

We had a friend who was our friend from early days, with whom we often pictured the changes that were to come upon our lives, and merrily imagined how we would speak, and walk, and think, and talk, when we came to be old. His destined habitation in the City of the Dead received him in his prime. Shall he be shut out from our Christmas remembrance? Would his love have so excluded us? Lost friend, lost child, lost parent, sister, brother, husband, wife, we will not so discard you! You shall hold your cherished places in our Christmas hearts, and by our Christmas fires; and in the season of immortal hope, and on the birthday of immortal mercy, we will shut out Nothing!

The winter sun goes down over town and village; on the sea it makes a rosy path, as if the Sacred tread were fresh upon the water. A few more moments, and it sinks, and night comes on, and lights begin to sparkle in the prospect. On the hill-side beyond the shapelessly-diffused town, and in the quiet keeping of the trees that gird the village-steeple, remembrances are cut in stone, planted in common flowers, growing in grass, entwined with lowly brambles around many a mound of earth. In town and village, there are doors and windows closed against the weather, there are flaming logs heaped high, there are joyful faces, there is healthy music of voices. Be all ungentleness and harm excluded from the temples of the Household Gods, but be those remembrances admitted with tender encouragement! They are of the time and all its comforting and peaceful reassurances; and of the history that reunited even upon earth the living and the dead; and of the broad beneficence and goodness that too many men have tried to tear to narrow shreds.

CHARACTERS

UNCLE CHILL, an avaricious, crabbed old man ; uncle to Michael.

CHRISTIANA, an old sweetheart of Michael's.

LITTLE FRANK, a diffident boy ; a cousin of Michael's.

MICHAEL, the "poor relation," and narrator of the story.

BETSY SNAP, a withered old woman, Uncle Chill's servant.

JOHN SPATTER, Michael's clerk, afterwards his partner.

THE
POOR RELATION'S STORY

He was very reluctant to take precedence of so many respected members of the family, by beginning the round of stories they were to relate as they sat in a goodly circle by the Christmas fire; and he modestly suggested that it would be more correct if "John our esteemed host" (whose health he begged to drink) would have the kindness to begin. For as to himself, he said, he was so little used to lead the way that really—— But as they all cried out here, that he must begin, and agreed with one voice that he might, could, would, and should begin, he left off rubbing his hands, and took his legs out from under his armchair, and did begin.

I have no doubt (said the poor relation) that I shall surprise the assembled members of our family, and particularly John our esteemed host to whom we are so much indebted for the great hospitality with which he has this day entertained us, by the confession I am going to make. But, if you do me the honour to be surprised at anything that falls from a person so unimportant in the family as I am, I can only say that I shall be scrupulously accurate in all I relate.

I am not what I am supposed to be. I am quite another thing. Perhaps before I go further, I had better glance at what I *am* supposed to be.

It is supposed, unless I mistake—the assembled members of our family will correct me if I do, which is very likely (here the poor relation looked mildly about him for contradiction); that I am nobody's enemy but my own. That I never met with any particular success in anything. That I failed in business because I was unbusiness-like and credulous

—in not being prepared for the interested designs of my partner. That I failed in love, because I was ridiculously trustful—in thinking it impossible that Christiana could deceive me. That I failed in my expectations from my uncle Chill, on account of not being as sharp as he could have wished in worldly matters. That, through life, I have been rather put upon and disappointed in a general way. That I am at present a bachelor of between fifty-nine and sixty years of age, living on a limited income in the form of a quarterly allowance, to which I see that John our esteemed host wishes me to make no further allusion.

The supposition as to my present pursuits and habits is to the following effect.

I live in a lodging in the Clapham Road—a very clean back room, in a very respectable house—where I am expected not to be at home in the day-time, unless poorly; and which I usually leave in the morning at nine o'clock, on pretence of going to business. I take my breakfast—my roll and butter, and my half-pint of coffee—at the old-established coffee-shop near Westminster Bridge; and then I go into the City—I don't know why—and sit in Garraway's Coffee House, and on 'Change, and walk about, and look into a few offices and counting-houses where some of my relations or acquaintance are so good as to tolerate me, and where I stand by the fire if the weather happens to be cold. I get through the day in this way until five o'clock, and then I dine: at a cost, on the average, of one and threepence. Having still a little money to spend on my evening's entertainment, I look into the old-established coffee-shop as I go home, and take my cup of tea, and perhaps my bit of toast. So, as the large hand of the clock makes its way round to the morning hour again, I make my way round to the Clapham Road again, and go to bed when I get to my lodging—fire being expensive, and being objected to by the family on account of its giving trouble and making a dirt.

Sometimes, one of my relations or acquaintance is so obliging as to ask me to dinner. Those are holiday occasions, and then I generally walk in the Park. I am a solitary man, and seldom walk with anybody. Not that I am avoided because I am shabby; for I am not at all shabby, having always a very good suit of black on (or rather Oxford mixture, which has the appearance of black and wears much better); but I have got into a habit of speaking low, and being rather